RISING TO THE RIM

Rising to the Rim

Poems by Carol Tyx

BRICK ROAD
POETRY PRESS

Cover: *Cereal Bowl & Newspaper*, painting by Marie Fox

Author photo: Jeff Koepp

Library of Congress Control Number: 2013940144

ISBN-13: 978-0-9835304-9-7

Published by Brick Road Poetry Press
P. O. Box 751
Columbus, GA 31902-0751
www.brickroadpoetrypress.com

Brick Road logo by Dwight New

To my father, Harry Servis Whitehouse,
who has risen over the rim
1921-2006

CONTENTS

I. GRAVITY

II. MORE WEIGHT

III. ENTERING THE FIRE

I. GRAVITY

Abundance

can almost kill you,
hanging your sheets
the first real day
of spring, before the official
pronouncement, when the sun
surprises with reckless warmth,
and even though your hands
stiffen holding wet cloth,
you keep fastening the pins
that hold you to this day,
trembling in the light.

Morning after Fog Series, North Shore

I. *Waking*

Overnight the fog has lifted
and color reappears—
green lake, blue sky restored.
Dressing for the day,
I keep looking at the lupines
just outside my window,
their little shoes
climbing the stalk,
the whole throng chanting
purple, purple, pink, pink.

II. *Breakfast on the Porch*

I feast on flowers—pansies,
snapdragons, lobelia—
the colors so vivid
I have to say them
in another language
to make them bright
enough: *amarillo, azul,*
rosa, morado.

III. *Paper, Rock, Butterfly*

I lean on the rock shelf
and listen to the loose
water sloshing below.
Quieted by the fog
the surf drowses,
only the thinnest of green lines
where the water lifts itself over
the outermost rock.
A butterfly, her wings
tucked in, sits near me.

IV. *Barefoot, Baretime*

As water flaps over my feet,
I feel a quickening
all the way up my legs;
the butterfly, still on the same rock,
opens and closes her wings.
Time takes off its shoes;
I can't find the beginning
or the ending of an hour,
rock and water
endlessly overlapping.

Red Tomato Rain

Rain all day running down the vines,

one red tomato hidden in a green cage,

a juicy heart. Tell me how a tomato turns

from green to red; tell me how one moment

stands out, luminous and wet.

In the Garden with Rilke

July. The garden fills
with the fullness of God: pale purple
hostas, blaring orange trumpet vines,
lemon-bright lilies.

Earlier, before color and shape unhinged me,
I was reading Rilke's *Book of Hours*:
I want to unfold.
Let no place in me hold itself closed,
For where I am closed, I am false.

Now the day is closing.
I take off my glasses, put down my pen,
trying to hold still, trying not to close,
trying to taste this late afternoon
light, this silken wind,
these luminous open bodies.

Birthday Morning

The first blossoms of the plum tree unfold,
the palest of pink among the purple leaves.

Barely awake, I feel my old cat curl over my navel,
wrinkled knot that tied me to this world.

Last night I dreamed a man who is lonely and kind
held me in his arms, and the holding was like

the first softening of the dark and when I opened
my eyes, the deep green of the grass

looked so lush I wanted to lie down in it
and wait for the sun to find me.

Yesterday I took a child out in a kayak.
He was scared, he said, but wanted to paddle.

I have been that child for a long time.
Across the alley, a bird pauses on a wire,

a still moment before flying into the day.
I take a breath: it is my birthday morning

and I am hungry for another year.

Gravity

Accept gravity as earth's gift,
pulling you into place,
keeping your feet to the ground
like a flattened ear
listening for the knowledge
of how the earth gives you
weight, even when you feel
empty.

You think you drift
away from the rest of us
so easily. Listen to the questions
pulling you in like a shepherd's crook:
Why has the earth drawn you
to her? Why does she refuse
to let go?

Falling

You ski for the first time
stiff-legged, stick-armed
remembering with each slight slope
how quickly speed on ice

gets out of control,
how you broke your collarbone
skating; but with each fall,
in spite of helpless

sprawling, twisted knee,
broken pole, you learn to be
less afraid, trusting the ground
to hold you, your awkwardness

part of flying through winter
woods where owls hoot at a twilight
falling faster than you.

Caring for Boots

I want to age like
a pair of old hiking boots:
tread rounded
but not bald,
stitches still firm,
toes holding curves
slightly flattened,
instep high, tongue
soft and loose as it
folds and unfolds,
dark cherry leather
cracked in the creases,
unlaced, spread-
eagled in the sun,
every pore soaking up
sweet mink oil.

December in Glen Helen

for J.M.

I wanted to hold his longing
and mine, make a bowl for it,
even if I knew the edge
had cracked, even if I knew
we can't hold anything.

So we took off our coats
and our gloves and our ordinary lives
and lay down in the snow
beside the thick trees.

I could have been a bear
poking my head out of sleep
to see if I was still alive,
then settling back, certain
winter would go on.

Border Sleep

After *chili rellenos* so big even the toothpicks
holding them together fall out, my son,
just turned father, needs a nap. I sweep

the kitchen, throw in another load of diapers
for the baby who has finally fallen asleep,
then slither onto the couch, thinking

Who would choose to live here? The overhead fan spins,
the paddles humming like the refrigerator
that never stops running. Outside, pods burst

and crackle and somehow the birds manage
to keep singing while the heat presses us flat
as tortillas. Dogs sprawl on the floor and

diapers stiffen on the line as I dream of
catching snowflakes on my tongue.
When the baby wakes up, the only thing

that can unpin us from sleep is the thought
of *raspas*, cold as packed snow; in a trance,
we imagine ice slicing through our burning lips.

When Loneliness Moves In

Start a daily practice, like flossing,
that keeps her from building up.
Fetch a tomcat to live with you
hoping he will catch her,
no more squeaking at night.

Climb her like stairs, stomp
one aching foot after another, panting
by the time you reach the top.

Chase her with the vacuum cleaner,
throw her against a wall, stuff her
in a ziplock bag in the refrigerator
where you will forget about her
until she fuzzes.

Or make the guest bed,
tuck in the flannel sheets,
offer the feather pillow,
tell her she can stay the night
and in the morning
call a taxi.

Love Poem for My Bladder

All the art of living lies in a fine mingling of letting go and holding on.
—Havelock Ellis

Sweetheart, we've been together
fifty-eight years—can you believe it—

and never a day without
the two of us. Some might call us

codependent, but is there
any other way? We're about as close

as we can get—when you hurt,
I hurt even worse.

Oh I know I can take you for granted,
forgetting to tell you how much I adore you,

your svelte curves, your amazing
flexibility, your capacity to have

and to hold. I know you get irritated—
overworked, underappreciated,

no vacation in all these years,
no retirement in sight even though

we both know you're wearing down,
leaking a little when I sneeze,

waking me to walk you to the bathroom—
but promise you'll never leave me.

I may sound desperate—I am—
I can't live without you.

At the Spoon River Rest Stop

I was having a hard time getting home,
floating above the earth,
a restless hovering that did not know
where to land, the rest stop full of ghosts,
my sons disappearing one winter
while I slumped in the car, feverish,
recently divorced; my relief
when they emerged from the woods
with tales of the ice-coated Spoon River.

It was the prairie that pulled me
back down. Like the fast-flitting swallowtail,
my spirit raced over the cropped grass,
then circled toward the prairie flowers,
drawn to their reckless color,
purple and gold and orange.

Or maybe it was the grasshopper,
the one that tapped me
on the forehead, knocked on me
like a door, and I knew
I could make it home.

Homage to My Red Bed

Through sheets of darkness
we sailed to a new world,
your red hull holding
my loneliness until
I woke up and knew
it was only the other side
of the world
and not the end.

I wore you like an old shoe
so comforting to slide into,
slightly longer than my toes,
enough room to spread out,
dents and dips fitting my form.
In the red bed I held onto rhyming,
one word spooned into the next.
Even though I was only one,
we were two, a whole body
of sound sleeping.

According to Feng Shui
in replacing you with this double bed
I'm sending out an invitation.
Yet I can hardly bear to carry you

out the door, you who carried me
over so many waves of longing.
I hope you'll find someone, too,
who fits your frame and remembers
you as red, no matter what color
you might take on.

Reading Hafiz on a
Cold Wednesday Morning

Hafiz wakes up early, eases down
his side of the double bed,
feeds the cat, kindles a fire,
puts the kettle on for tea,
rolls up the shade and sings
to the crystal blue light.

Although it is not my birthday,
he reads me a poem that tastes like
a present, a perfectly ripe pineapple;
when he strokes my foot, I know this is not
a signal about sex, even though he is purring
as he caresses my toes, pulls off
my pajamas, and hands me my most
comfortable clothes.

Dancing with my scalp,
he braids my hair and wraps the ends
with kisses. While I brush my teeth,
he scrapes the ice off my car,
turns on the heater, pulls the hat he knit
over my nose and tells me
how good it looks on me.

As I back down the driveway
he shoveled last night,
Hafiz slips back into bed, where
he will be waiting for my return.

God Comes as a Cat

In the belly of the night
when time's ribs make
a bubble in which we float,

you crawl in bed
beside me. At first your body
thrums, an outboard motor

to move us through
the deep; somewhere we slip
into silence, where we

drift for hours, your
padded paw resting
against my cheek,

and when darkness
spits us out on the beach
of morning, I want to remember

the heft of your body
across my shoulder.

Around the Curve

Once I came around a curve
and fell into a profusion

of wild white roses
swaying in the sun.

Their sudden sweetness
in the hot noon air

trembled like incense
rising in the woods.

Years before, I came around a curve
and hit a car while turning

left onto a gravel road.
White dust shook all around us,

and now you: are you a rose,
a car, or something

utterly new?

Water Boy

for Benjamin Byrd Tyx

At eight months
he's all motion
hurling himself headfirst
into sand, aiming
for the dog dishes,
stalking the cat.

At the fountain
he's a torrent, hanging
on his father's hand, careening
toward the liquid lines
spurting up at least twice
his height.

He staggers—
he can't even walk
yet he's running—
dragging his dad
through curtains of silver.

He's one of many
kids as unpredictable as
the water, leaping up,

falling down—streaks
of energy—kids in swimsuits,
dresses, even long pants;
he's the only one in diapers
but no one notices, all bathed
in naked joy.

Extravagance

Maybe you've seen it—
a summer so wet and wild
the flowers have gone crazy
blooming in a thousand colors—
to list them would take
a year and then some.

Even the stalks can't bear
their own beauty, lilies
crashing into each other,
phlox bending with their own weight,
zinnias toppling.

Our eyes stagger—
rush hour in our optic nerve—
but we must keep going,
plowing through glory
even if we come to a full stop,
even if we fall to our knees.

Rising to the Rim

The easiest way to make sure
you love someone well is to
love everything, but we know
how hard that is, don't we?

So maybe it is better to think
of something simple, with sides,
like a cereal bowl. Even
big ones aren't much larger

than your hand. Yet so many mornings,
a lifetime if you're lucky, you might be
reading the newspaper, or telling the dog
you'll go for a walk soon

and when you look across
the table there will be a bowl
to match yours, milk rising
to the rim, another chance to learn

how to love everything.

For a Boy and His Father
in San Pedro Frío, Colombia

Every morning I watch them climb
the hill and sit on a plank bench at the hostel,
ready to do the most human thing.

It is cold and the boy leans into his father,
his head tucked as if under a wing.
The boy's eyes are open, but he sits so still

he seems to be asleep. Then, as if waking up,
he pulls a spoon from the rack and holds it
upright, like a flower. Carefully, he lays

the spoon down and reaches for another,
sliding it toward his father. When the soup comes,
the father offers a spoonful of broth.

The boy shakes his head, his mouth closed.
Tome, the father says gently, *tome*, and like a bird,
the boy opens his mouth and the father smiles.

The boy pinches off a nub of bread and lifts it
to his father's mouth. The man takes the bread,
his lips brushing the boy's fingers.

The boy smiles, and even though my soup has not arrived, I feel warm and full.

Hungering

The disciples were slow to learn
but quick to follow. Maybe they hungered,
like we do, for lives beyond the daily catch;

maybe those who risked
setting out to sea each morning
knew the necessity

of heading for deeper water
if they had any hope of a fuller net,
one that could feed five thousand;

or maybe their first thoughts were smaller,
a walk with friends, a cup of wine,
a word from this teacher

and before they knew it, these fisherfolk
had become farmers, plowed up
their hearts so parables

they didn't quite understand
could take root.

Seeding

Melons are easy,
cream-colored slivers
that slide through
your fingers into
soil blocks.

Cabbage are harder,
round, rolling
across your palm
like tiny ball bearings.

But lettuce takes the cake,
weightless nubs, specks
of dust that cling
to your hand.

Carla teaches me
how to wet the end
of a pencil to catch
a single seed,
but I still can't see
anything dropping

into the soil. Yet
within a week,
from smaller than small,
the kingdom of lettuce rises.

The Poet in the Raspberry Patch

They often evade you
  hiding under leaves
    dangling just out of reach.

You have to think like a squirrel
  tilt your head, try upside down
    stretch to the limit

push toward the center
  thrust through thorns
    pluck one by one.

Ripeness is all
  just the right shade of red
    a little give but still solid.

Be ready for surprises
  what you missed yesterday
    waits for you today.

II. MORE WEIGHT

Starlite Motel

I stood in the doorway
taking in the single room:
rumpled blanket on gray tile,
open bag of chips, clothes
spilling out of a paper sack,
naked light bulb.

You asked if I wanted to come in.
I wanted to shut my eyes
but I knew I would have to see it,
even say it—separation—
if we were ever to move
toward a light less raw.

I couldn't say your name yet,
but I took a step inside while you
tied your shoes, your movements
both strange and familiar,
each hand picking up an end
while I waited to see what might happen
when you stood up. We didn't touch.

When you climbed in the car, you fumbled
with the seatbelt; my feet barely reached

the pedals. Staring straight ahead
I let out the clutch and we lurched
toward the highway.

Dream Dancing

You were wearing your blue Hawaiian shirt
and a pair of dancing slippers
while you played a flute,

the notes falling over my head
like a soft rain. You wanted me
to dance with you

like we did the night before I left
so I held out my hands but your fingers
had become charred embers

and I backed away, barely able
to breathe, the music turning
to smoke. You kept playing,

your fingertips charged with a light
I could still see as I fell
into a basement apartment

five hundred miles away
filled with unfamiliar furniture.

What Is the Grass?

Mr. Lawrence, whose grass
turns tawny in November, waters
his golden grass in his undershirt,
white belly bulging over his belt,
water arcing. We roll like dogs
on his lawn, stubbly, prickled,
so different from ours.

Now the hose has fallen, water
sliding down the black driveway,
and my mother, who is hanging sheets,
my mother who always knows what to do,
hollers *Harry, Harry*, and my father,
who never runs, runs from the garage
across our soft green grass.

My father, who never does anything
except shave in just an undershirt,
pulls off his plaid shirt and now Mr. Lawrence
looks like he is sleeping, his eyes closed,
the shirt tucked around him
like a blanket, and my father,
who always smiles, is not smiling,
his arms white as bones sticking out

from his undershirt, and I worry
when he disappears into the ambulance

that he'll never come back,
not thinking at all about
Mr. Lawrence, his lawn
getting stiffer, water still pouring
down the driveway.

Grandmother's Lament

I kept thinking my presence could help,
holding him close while I circled

the yard chanting I'm here, you're loved,
and when it was clear that my love was not enough

I called on the green world, naming each flower,
tree, and cloud, but nothing could distract him

from his full-throttled agony—only
absence, finally, could speak to him,

only alone in his crib could he be at home,
resting, at last, in his inconsolable grief.

After a Brain Injury

for P.M.

What happens when the mind jams
like a finger, bone against bone,
no room to bend, thought pressed
to thought, words stuck to themselves,
cupboard doors swollen shut in July
with no way to reach the iced tea mix?

Restlessness

You walk for hours on the edge of town
as if open space might allow whatever you are looking for
to appear or disappear so you can stop
looking for it; neither happens.

As you keep walking you imagine your brain
like a Gordian knot: you want to become the ruler
of yourself but splitting your head will hurt
and besides, you know from years

of trying to unravel this restlessness
that it's never that neat, pieces
pulling you in so many directions
it's a wonder you can walk anywhere.

Someone calls but you aren't home,
you never want to be home and yet
you wish you could settle in.
*Why in the world is she walking
so late at night?* the caller asks.
You wish you could answer
but the knot cannot be untied
by this kind of question.

You have not brought any water.
You think you should be thirsty
but if you are, you don't know it.

You keep walking,
afraid of what might happen
if you stop. Afraid of what
might happen if you don't.

Another Pole

Lying on the white sheets

he reminds me of a man

on an ice floe breaking loose,

unsure how he arrived

on this austere continent.

How fast are you drifting?

I want to ask. He closes his eyes

as my sister announces

she's called an ambulance.

His eyes still shut,

my father grates,

I'm ready to go,

in the half voice

he has left,

one vocal cord

already sliced off.

Even before

they carry him out,

he sounds far away.

Zero at the Bone

Last night on the phone
my son told me he had left his four-month-old son
in the car, forgetting he was there.

In the checkout line he remembered
and abandoning his cart, flung himself
through the line.

The police had opened the door
and the baby was quiet,
but they wouldn't let my son

touch his child. I don't know
what happened inside him
or the baby as he watched his father

dissolve, then reappear, crying,
and I don't know what to say on the phone
murmuring, *Oh sweetie, oh sweetie,*

words I never use, words my father said to me
when I stuck my hand in the blades of a lawnmower
and I cried in the grass holding the flesh together.

Things My Mother Can't Find
after Breaking Her Pelvis

Her apartment: the recipe for spinach quiche

on the kitchen counter, the spinach

in the freezer. Her nail file,

the orange pound cake she bought

at the bake sale, the floss threader

for her bridge, her checkbook

with Clara Catherine in the corner.

Her cane: if only she had her cane

she could hoist herself

out of this wheelchair and

onto the commode and

what do you mean she can't

have her cane until her hip heals?

E-pisss-co-pal-ian: the word her best friend

passed on to her before she died

that helps you pee when your aide is watching

and you can't get things started.

Her name: *Clara*, a young woman

with a West African accent calls out.

My mother stares at her smeared plate.

Clara's my grandmother, she tells her tablemates.

I'm Katie, have been for years.

How to call for help: push the button.

Where's the button? Around your neck.

What do I do with it? Push it.

I already pushed it. Is the light on?

No. So what should you do?

Push the button. Yes.

Mother Math

She'll tell you herself
she was never good at math,
the x's and y's jumping around
her day as if she were trying
to read without glasses.

In the dark she dresses:
blue-striped blouse, tan slacks,
new shoes with Velcro straps.
So far the numbers add up, but now
a missing purse—she put it on the table
last night—and a missing person,
her son-in-law, who should be here
to take her to the dentist.
At four am, she calls her daughter.

Next month?
That can't be right.
Her daughter tells her to write
plans for the day in a notebook.
She can't find the notebook,
or the book she needs to return
to the library, or the library,
such a lovely collection lost,
one more unsolved equation.

Leaving Her Son in Indiana

He will live by himself
in a town where he does not
fit in. She knows what this is like

and because she does not want him
to come home to a cold house
she crouches on all fours and blows

into the black box, where a big wedge
of wood she managed to cram inside
is not burning. So even though it is time

to leave, she continues hurling her breath
into the mouth of the stove
wanting to keep this fire alive

if only for a few more hours.

Final Boarding

You thought we were returning,
following the same trajectory back
as we pulled away from the gate
and rushed down the runway.
By the time we nosed
into the sky you were asleep,
your hand locked over mine.
I leaned against the exit door,
tired but restless, the weight
of trying to lift you into my life
too much.

We hadn't quarreled at your sister's;
we'd been sleepy and slow
in the weekend-long drizzle
but when we took off, I knew
I'd never fly with you again.

How do we know what we know?
The plane was a match striking
the sky, burning up and up
until where we had been
disappeared, the distance
roaring in my ears.

Dwindling

for R. T.

Before his eyes, his daughter
is disappearing, at midnight
climbing the kitchen stepladder,
reaching for something
he can't see from the hallway,
readying herself for dawn in the woods
he thinned, where her prayers or meditations
or whatever she does there day after day
trail through the trees. He wishes
he were the trees; she has stopped
speaking to him.

In the early morning darkness
he pauses at her door to warn her
about thunderstorms; she slides him a note—
please, no interruptions—and later,
a few more words folded up—
your sins are forgiven. He's not sure
what his sins are, but he longs for his daughter
at daybreak, her back to him as she washes
the yellow yolk off his plate. He wishes

he were the egg, her hand reaching
toward him; he fears she is the egg,
her bright center washing away.

Later, as he pulls the tarp
over the woodpile, he stands
in the rain remembering
how she helped him bring in the wood
they burned in the stove last winter,
all of it gone now.

Holly Jo

You surprised us by living
eight years with only the nub
of a brain. They told me
you couldn't see or hear or feel
but I swear you smiled once
when I said you had hair like mine,
a rich auburn, our one good feature.

I thought when you died
I'd be relieved, that I could let this
longing for numbness slide into
the ground. Even before
you were born I had stopped
using, but not a day passes
I don't want to swallow something—
anything—to fill that emptiness.

Sometimes in my dreams
you see me and don't turn away.
I always hope you'll talk to me;
you never do.

Hands

When my student, nineteen
and outside Alabama
for the first time, comes
to my home in rural Indiana,
he brings a bottle of soap.

When I ask why, he tells me
I might think his hands
aren't clean enough to handle
the cookies we're making
for the Black History Month reading.

Looking at Luther's hands—big, long-fingered,
the color of strong black coffee,
the palms gloriously pink, unlike mine,
a yellowish orange mottled with blue—

I remember the school superintendent
in Ernest Gaines' *A Lesson Before Dying*
inspecting the hands of students in the quarter
and the teacher's throttled anger.

Taking the bowl in my arms,
I beat and beat the stiff dough,
then pass the thick ball to Luther.
He flours the counter, then rolls the dough

paper thin, his hands sliding lightly
over the smooth surface, that surface
carrying so much more weight than its
tissue-thin layers should have to bear.

Chains

Before they chained him to the truck
they spray painted his face black,
the molecules of paint sliding
into his lungs, the darkness
of that night now inside him.

Revving up the truck, they dragged him,
laying down a wavy red line
as the body of James Byrd
zigzagged back and forth.
A set of dentures popped out.

A mile down Huff Creek Road
the body swung around a bend
and hit a culvert. The blackened head
sheered off.

When mortician Dorie Coleman and his father,
who knew every black man in Jasper,
picked up the head, and two miles further
the body, they had no idea
who was riding with them.

And now that we know, what are we to do

with this terrible sundering, this body

broken for what, this history

chained to us?

In the Vukovar Rubbish Pit

This group, she surmises,
came straight from the hospital,
patients still in their pajamas,
bandages wrapped around rotting
flesh, one corpse with a sheaf
of X-rays hidden under
his robe. On alert for what
a family might recognize
she bags and labels remnants
of clothing—nightgowns,
underwear, socks—pushing
against the anonymity of
mass killing. She's young,
convinced that this evidence
will indict the killers.

It's not the smell
or the maggots that
undo her as she scrapes
dirt from under a shoulder.
It's the crutches. How
he must have teetered
to the pit, lurching

on the uneven ground,

how he heard the bullets

behind him as, holding himself

upright, his arms went slack

before he tipped over, all around him

bodies raining.

For a moment

she's flying with him, all the careful

precision of her work left behind,

only the crushing weight

of bodies piling up.

Notes From Afar

The week after 9/11
I wasn't there

to hear the song that exploded
from the piano, the notes

jumping from buildings
into the arms of strangers

who fell to the ground
and crawled back up

as different people.
The man in the second row

remembers the ash
how it fell

for days, gritty and gray,
fell out of television sets

into living rooms, onto
kitchen floors and cracked

lips and mixed with the grief
floating in the air.

A girl in the back
recalls the silence

how her students stared
at the television as words

fell off the blackboard,
the classroom cracking

like an egg.
A woman listening

from the hallway remembers
watching the smoke

rise on the screen,
how she couldn't

turn off the water,
soapsuds overflowing

the sink, her hand
trapped underneath,

or that's what I heard
since the week after 9/11

I was no longer there
to hear my son, who writes songs,

sound this gasping,

the collapsing that was

no longer mine.

Turkey Vultures

Along the rocky slope of the Coralville dam
the turkey vultures hunch, solid as stones,
dark and dense.

Above me wings dipped in white soar, so smooth
they appear weightless, feathers
made of air.

I keep watching the rock-riven clumps:
I want to see the moment they rise, how it happens,
how heaviness

lifts itself and floats into the sky. But they only
teeter from rock to rock, their wings tucked
around their secrets.

III. ENTERING THE FIRE

Yoga Practice

In yoga there are no
mountaintops, only the daily
practice of climbing into
each pose as far as you can.
Think in decades,
our teacher urges us:
ten years may be the start
of understanding one
of the less complicated poses.

So we practice our dogs
and cows, our camels
and peacocks; we forget
our Sanskrit and remember
tree, boat, bridge;
we try not to groan,
to sigh, to laugh
at our awkwardness,
our stiffness, our craziness
to think we might someday be
a crane or a one-legged king pigeon.

And at the end
when we lie in corpse pose

trying not to think

how hungry we are

or how our legs ache

and our teacher tells us

be content, we know we need

to practice that, too.

Learning God Like Spanish

I learn God like I learn Spanish,

which is to say slowly,

with a lot of repetition.

The language of God

is not my native tongue.

Over and over I must practice

the most basic conjugations:

to love in the singular

and the plural,

in first and second

and third person.

Shedding

He makes it look so easy, shedding
hair after hair as they slide to the surface
and float across the couch, not even noticing
the bits of himself coming loose.

Remnants

My mother's eyes close, but her fingers
keep tracking across the page,
her lips moving as she turns
the pages backwards. When I ask her
what she's doing, she says,
I'm thinking what I'm going to do.
Her finger points to a circled word:
we've got something like this
and we couldn't figure it out.
As I jot down the sentence, noting
it's half in the present, half
in the past, she stares at my hand.
I don't have a pencil.
I dig in my bag, find notepad
and pen. *Now what am I going to do?*
Her eyelids flutter, the pen falls
from her hand. The question hangs
like laundry left on the line
long after it's dry.

The Time of Falling Leaves

I remember a Sunday morning
during a sermon when the leaves
on the elm let loose and we all sighed as if
God had swept down from heaven.

The pastor thought she had said
something profound,
and perhaps she had, but if so,
we missed it, our minds emptied
of all our ideas of God.

Below the Grass

At last the Japanese beetles
have lived out their lives
and the roses and raspberries
can breathe again,
new leaves stretching out
even in September.

Yet death is not the end:
below the grass, the next generation
sleeps, grateful for
some lover of the grass
that has provided such a quiet spot
to lean and loaf until
the summer sun calls up
their hunger.

Late Raspberry Season

The leaves speckle,
pull into themselves;

the cane tips turn brown.
Yet the berries come,

smaller, but just as sweet,
hiding under a leaf or tucked

in the grass, wine-colored
thimbles just big enough to fit

on a finger. It's October.
The wet spell has passed,

the moldy weeks with
rotted red flesh.

We know the first frost
will march in under cover

of darkness, but we don't know
when, so we keep hurrying,

every afternoon filling

our pails with last minute gifts

from the berry gods.

Jamming

begins with whole notes
   round and blue
      and ripe,

stemmed washed
   mashed measured
      sugared.

Warming up slow, heat builds to a
   blue roiling, a tornado
      hefting a line, bending

what was solid to
   syrup, molten riff
      jumping, jiving

nothing held back,
   burners blaring
      glass too hot to touch.

Tongs lift lids
   over hot sweet blue.
      Listen for the seal

that last note preserving

   all that has gone before

     in one final

ping.

The Final Hoop

Ever since my sister tells me
you can't turn over,
I know you are turning inward,
the list of things you need
to pay attention to
dwindling.

Still, your heart
races: where are you
trying to go
in such a hurry?

Just yesterday,
my sister reports,
you were joking with the doctor
about the basketball game on TV,
and now you are the one
poised at the line, ready
to pass through the net.

In your last wakeful
moments, you call my sister
your burial keeper. Perhaps this

is all the living can be to you now,

making sure you slide easy

as you swoosh through the tunnel,

all those hands waiting for you.

Where I Come From

In the center
of an old black and white
I found at the funeral,
my dad cradles me,
his tanned arms looped
around me, my white sweater
blending into his t-shirt;
we're both smiling,
awash in light.

He's so young,
his face full, his hair
shiny; I have only
a dot of hair, my ears
curving out like his.

On the back he has written
my original name
with his fountain pen,
Carol Ann Whitehouse.

I remember that pen,
how its tiny silver arm

pumped blue into the long
body, filling and emptying.

Narrative Tantrum

I don't want the story to end,

I want these lives to go on and on.

Happy or not, I want forever.

I hate the moment of closing

the cover—when nothing else

can happen—lowering the lid and

sliding the silent body on the shelf.

I never want to read another book,

it won't be as good as this one,

only this story matters.

Corpse Pose

Give yourself plenty of room, she says,
start with your knees bent, then slowly
let them go until you are only

a piece of silk floating down to accept
the support beneath you. Let your fingers
uncurl; soften any tightness in your jaw

and if a thought occurs, let it be
like a cloud passing through your mind,
each exhalation taking you closer

to nothing. She makes it sound so easy
and I hope it is, like sliding
a boat into water.

I Would Like to Go to Heaven in a Chalupa

with the wind blowing my reluctance

behind me and the deep smell of dark water,

stopping at every scraggly port

to pick up more passengers

and burlap sacks of fish, riding

the line where the river meets the sky

while we eat empanadas and fresh mangoes

and squeeze yet one more body in the boat,

the water slapping against the bow

as the driver ferries us from one shore

to the other.

Sunflowers II

after Mary Oliver's "The Sunflowers"

Come with me
  into the field of sunflowers,
    their heads heavy, their gold gone

to mustard. All summer
  their tall stalks were
    busy highways.

Now that part of the work
  is done and they stand still,
    heads bowed, thick with seeds.

I remember how you
  loved seeds, how you stood
    amazed at their smallness,

whole beings inside,
  carrying the knowledge
    of who they are,

everything they need
  to become
    already present,

those long days

lived in the light

leading them.

Preparing the Beans

One by one, like beads,
the beans slide through
my fingers under the cold water.

Solid as stones, they have lain
in my cupboard for months
waiting for this rain
to wash over them.

Now in the dark while I sleep
they begin to soften,
each cell opening

a door, letting in
a crowd of wet guests.
The very walls bow out,
the ceiling lifts—

all this even before
entering the fire.

Acknowledgments

My gratitude to the editors of the following magazines where some of these poems (or previous versions of them) first appeared:

A Celebration of Women and Aging, The University of Nebraska at Omaha: "Birthday Morning" and "Caring for Boots"

Anderbo: "Zero at the Bone"

Iowa City Poetry in Public Project: "Shedding" and "Red Tomato Rain"

Pirene's Fountain: "Corpse Pose"

Poetry East: "Narrative Tantrum"

RHINO: "Preparing the Beans"

Tenth Muse: "Learning God Like Spanish" and "What Is the Grass?"

the Aurorean: "In the Garden With Rilke"

Water-Stone Review: "Chains"

Yankee: "Gravity"

About the Author

Carol Tyx grew up in Cincinnati, Ohio. After a decade of employment in special education, Carol returned to her first loves—reading and writing—initially at Wright State University and then at The University of Iowa. Her chapbook, *The Fifty Poems*, bears witness to these transitions. More recently, her work has appeared in *RHINO*, *Poetry East*, *Water~Stone Review,* and Iowa City's Poetry in Public project.

Currently, Carol lives in Iowa City where she tends her raspberry patch, helps out at a local CSA, practices yoga and mindfulness, fumbles with big questions amidst a faith community, and teaches writing and literature at Mount Mercy University. She has two sons, a daughter by marriage, and two grandchildren. On any given day you might find her cooking with kale, contra dancing, or standing on her head.

Please visit Brick Road Poetry Press at our web site
for more poetry collections
that will entertain, amuse, and edify:
www.brickroadpoetrypress.com

In the following pages, samples are provided from
Chosen by **Toni Thomas**
&
Tracing the Lines by **Susanna Lang**

Chosen by Toni Thomas

ISBN-13: 978-0-9835304-1-1

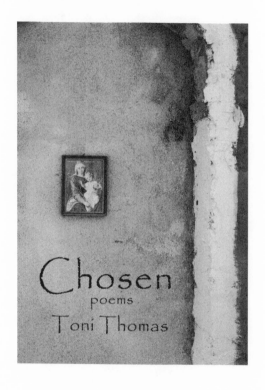

From *Chosen* by Toni Thomas

While the Car Crash Was Still Receding from Her Mind's Imaginary Aquarium

Majestic—maybe that's what she wanted
dangerous even
as if bad had its aspirin-coated appeal
dark licorice stories to tell
like the one-eyed psychic
wedged in black
who lived up past the sound
had a cue of customers waiting out
games of solitaire by the door.

It was her second life
after the car crash.
The plastic surgeon's apocalyptic
calling to reconstruct and stitch back her face.
The months of white bandages, work leave
marriage separation, the one-room studio apartment
she succored with her prayer book
the exact morsels of dinner by the bed.
Nobody could accuse her of being fat anymore
or materialistic or pedestrian as neat married
women in pantyhose clutching stiff umbrellas
to ward off the rain.
Her ecclesiastical life burning.
Sweet on the bread sticks.
How many cups of tea, cigarettes
to collapse a day
wring it out white eyelet
on the sloped clothesline.

Everything kept raining
down on her—
God and light
unimaginable suitors

stilted houses
under which the sea keeps heaving.

From *Chosen* by Toni Thomas

We Made Love in the Japanese Garden

the two of us loitering
in the corner
away from the tourists.
Lulled amid the bamboo screens
pools of carp, gabled roof lines.
Two geese flying.
The drip drip drip of slow water
from the bamboo pipe
rupturing the pond's smooth skin.

You said you'd love me forever
but did not want this child.
She of the secret bessoming.
I made a pact with God
that what was lost would someday
come back as hyacinth.

Eight years later it takes hours
to land in Beijing
make the journey south to you.
You are beautiful, my daughter
four-years-old, love tangerines
are ringworm infested, have a bald spot
an island where lustrous
black tresses long to be.
I have painted you stories for your
journey to me.
The dark sea, the surreptitious boat
me trying to reach you.
My sad hands empty as pigeons.
The hummingbird's cool breath.

You speak Cantonese.
At first the body's own language of love

must make a nest for us.
Later, my small painting pegged to your wall
you ask why it took so long
to reach you.
I talk about big squalls, shipwrecks
nights with no stars in them
the boat with its capsizable keel
how I bargained with God
to keep a watchful eye on you—
oldest girl
three and a half long years in the orphanage
told God that I would treasure you always
like the orange carp in the happy pond

told God I would make good
on my treasonous past
the man who won his sensible way
over my vestibules
the secret transgression
the knowledge of fishes.
That what is lost
I shall will back to us
as psalm.

From *Chosen* by Toni Thomas

The Grey Eye of Success Casts a Halo
over the Coast's Otherwise Sodden Geometry

The nights here are calm as
cursed cotton
calculated school rooms.
Everyone asleep in the satin sheets
of their beds.
Transients marooned in another
coast town
where the coffee is cheap
and the streets are lined with a string
of rundown bungalows
almost nobody owns.

I will be here a week.
As if placid is calling me.
People who saunter with their french pastries
reliable second homes.

One morning will I wake up
stunned by the sea's benevolence
the trees' refusal to grow old here?
Does the moon ever miss a beat
desert her well-off husband
and run?

Tracing the Lines by Susanna Lang
ISBN-13: 978-0-9835304-6-6

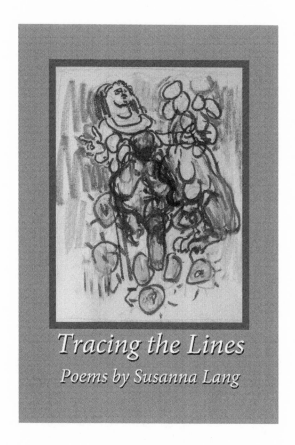

Tracing the Lines

Poems by Susanna Lang

From *Tracing the Lines* by Susanna Lang

Remembering

> *What has kept the world safe...[has]been memory.*
> —John Hersey

But we forget, don't we?
Not what happened, but the thickness of it.
The rough edges of the table
on the café terrace, moisture
beading on your glass. The way the woman
who would become your wife
kept pushing her hair off her forehead.
The sound of a cicada spinning to its death on the sidewalk,
a papery sound, like someone thumbing through a book.

Think of the man who returns
a year after the five-day war
in which his house was burned.
What's left of it
still stands on the corner, so he can search
among the black and crumbled stones,
the splintered table legs, for the photo
he didn't expect to find—
photo of a woman, her hair swept back
in a style no one wears anymore. He'd forgotten
that she used to wear her hair that way,
as he's forgotten the stretched feel of his skin
in the heat of the flames he watched from across the street,
though he'd tell you that's the one thing
he would remember forever.

From *Tracing the Lines* by Susanna Lang

Night Letters

> *I cannot tell if the day*
> *is ending, or the world, or if*
> *the secret of secrets is inside me again.*
> —Anna Akhmatova

Written on the undersides of leaves, along their veins;

written on the thin sheet of water laid over stones in the creek;

laid down with the saxophone track on the album
Sonny named for those telegrams with the special
night rate, 50 words for the price of 10—

the news you waited all night to read, or the news
you dreaded each time you answered the door.

Written on the back of an envelope returned as undeliverable
and then folded and forgotten in a pocket, sent to the wash.

Nailed to the door, for you to find in the morning,
when you finally understand what woke you in the night
and what could come pounding at your door another night.

What he wrote in response, what she revised and copied herself,
what someone left in the mailboxes of those who would know
what to do with it, who would know to recopy what had been written
and pass it on, mailbox to mailbox through an unbroken series of nights:

I've written down the words that I've not dared to speak.

Left as a clue to the location of what was buried
decades ago, so that someone else can brush the light crumbly soil
from these bones, reconstructing what happened at the very end,
what was nearly disappeared.

From *Tracing the Lines* by Susanna Lang

Dead Letters

> *…cries like dead letters sent*
> *to dearest him that lives alas! away.*
> —Gerard Manley Hopkins

Marked *Recipient Unknown*—
the numbers reversed, or if the numbers were correct
the street was wrong, someone wrote West instead of North.

Sent to an address misheard, misunderstood,
impossible to imagine from the other side of the globe—
Sterite or *Stiejt* instead of *Street.*

Addressed but not delivered, not deliverable,
sent to the Dead Letter Office to be destroyed
after any items of value had been removed from the envelope,
the paper (smudged, edges crinkled, saturated with ink
and with the words someone had rehearsed
for days before committing to them) sold for scrap.

Addressed in a dead language, a language no one speaks anymore,
though a few remember hearing it spoken when they were young:
Apalachee, Galice dialect, Miami-Illinois, Nooksack,
or the Aka-Bo known only by an old woman in India
who died this year, who survived the tsunami in 2004
because she understood when the earth spoke to her
and so knew to climb a tree high above the floods.

Mailed to a son gone silent, his exact location unknown:
The lost are like this.
His last place of employment written carefully
on the outside of the envelope.

That letter did arrive at Number 4 Barrington Street
and the prodigal son wrote back to his mother,
a resurrection chronicled, with a great deal of satisfaction,
at the Dead and Revived Letter Office.

From *Tracing the Lines* by Susanna Lang

Tracing the Lines

There are lines you can trace like rivers in a geography,
those faint blue lines that wander back and forth across borders,
Dnister, "the close river," and Dnieper, "the river on the far side,"
rising in one country and draining in another. The line
of my son's jaw, so much like his uncle's jaw, or his great grandfather
who died while my mother was still a child, who rarely enters her stories
but sits squarely before the camera in his wedding photo,
his wife's hand resting on his shoulder, his jaw lifted in pride.
They left their river, a story told too often, to escape the soldiers—
not what you would expect to read in my son's English
Dissenter blue eyes, legacy of another set of ancestors, another
line on the map. *We do not come from mud,* a caption
beneath the photo of a family bringing the long dead
out from their crypts, narrow bundles tied with strips of cloth,
raised up so they can dance and offer advice and join
in the feast before they are wrapped in new cloths
and returned: *we come from these bodies.* My son
comes from these bodies, dressed in their most formal clothes
for the photo, the embroidered bodice, the starched collar, the tie
with a sheen to it, the string of pearls. Their lips are closed,
their eyes focused on the camera with its slow shutter,
but in a moment the photographer will turn away, and these bodies
will be ready to dance, they will have something to say.

Our Mission

The mission of Brick Road Poetry Press is to publish and promote poetry that entertains, amuses, edifies, and surprises a wide audience of appreciative readers. We are not qualified to judge who deserves to be published, so we concentrate on publishing what we enjoy. Our preference is for poetry geared toward dramatizing the human experience in language rich with sensory image and metaphor, recognizing that poetry can be, at one and the same time, both familiar as the perspiration of daily labor and as outrageous as a carnival sideshow.

Also Available from Brick Road Poetry Press

www.brickroadpoetrypress.com

Dancing on the Rim by Clela Reed

Possible Crocodiles by Barry Marks

Pain Diary by Joseph D. Reich

Otherness by M. Ayodele Heath

Drunken Robins by David Oates

Damnatio Memoriae by Michael Meyerhofer

Lotus Buffet by Rupert Fike

The Melancholy MBA by Richard Donnelly

Two-Star General by Grey Held

Chosen by Toni Thomas

Etch and Blur by Jamie Thomas

Water-Rites by Ann E. Michael

Bad Behavior by Michael Steffen

Tracing the Lines by Susanna Lang

About the Prize

The Brick Road Poetry Prize, established in 2010, is awarded annually for the best book-length poetry manuscript. Entries are accepted August 1st through November 1st. The winner receives $1000 and publication. For details on our preferences and the complete submission guidelines, please visit our website at www.brickroadpoetrypress.com.